The Tackle

Poems about the community,
the deep sea fishing and the
rugby of Hessle Road in Hull

**Sue Houlston
and
Terry Ireland**

Contents

Boulevard Heroes 5
The origins of rugby 7
Boulevard Farewell 9
Jack Harrison VC 11
Boulevard Heaven 13
Stan Cowan 15
Challenge Cup 16
Sammy Lloyd 18
Threepenny Stand 20
Lament for a Lost Player 21
Ted Capes 23
The Faithful 25
The Boulevard 2015 26
Old Faithful 28
Three Day Millionaires 31
Big Lil - 1968 33
Jonesy 35
Post Cod War Blues – Epitaph 37
Biography 39
To Skipper Pete 41
Post Cod War Blues Part 1 43
Fishgate Market 45
Post Cod War Blues - A mouthful of ashes 46
Lunch At The Sailmakers 48
Sidewinder Blues 51
Lord Line 53

2

Foreword

Until the death of the fishing industry following the Cod Wars with Iceland, Hull, a maritime city, boasted one of the largest deep sea fishing fleets in the world.

The fishing community was mainly centered around the Hessle Road area which borders the river and the docks. At the same time, the city boasted two top class rugby league teams. The city is split by the river and loyalty to each team tended to follow that geographical split. Hull FC is based in West Hull and as such has always been the team of choice for the fishing community.

Deep sea fishing was a hazardous occupation. Over the 150 year history of fishing in the city, some ten thousand lives were lost to this hard and dangerous life in unforgiving Arctic seas.

The rugby team still thrives but the fishing industry is, sadly, gone. What remains of the docks is just an area of dereliction awaiting the developers hand.

These poems are at times emotional, sad, wistful or humorous. They are a nostalgic look back to times past and a tribute to a very special people.

Sue Houlston and Terry Ireland
Hull 2015

Rugby

Sue Houlston

Boulevard Heroes

I was born just near Craven Park
Well that was really quite hard
Cos my family across all generations
Attended the Boulevard

We never reckoned much to Rovers
Though we could have walked it and saved the fare
But we preferred our rugby league
Across the river just over there

I saw Mick Crane and Knocker Norton
The finest loose forwards of all
And from an earlier generation
John Whiteley a wizard with the ball

I saw the Drake Twins weaving their magic
Saw the Kiwis, saw a young Lee Crooks
Dave Topliss, Richard Horne, Vince Farrar
And more in the record books

I'll never forget Sammy Lloyd
Peter Sterling or Stevie Prescott
Clive Sullivan, Tommy Harris, Arthur Keegan
Greg Mackie or lovely Mick Scott

And back in the mists of time
Stands Jack Harrison VC
He scored 52 tries in one season
Still a record at Hull FC

And later there was Joe Oliver
They say in 1936
Old Faithful was first sung for him
When he scored between the sticks

Cowboy Baxter was so short-sighted
He'd tackle anything above the grass
He once tackled the roller at the edge of the pitch
Before it could get in a pass

These are just some of my favourites
Among the players at Hull FC
And there are so many more
Who have meant a lot to me

We never reckoned much to Rovers
We could have walked it – it's not very hard
But we preferred our rugby
With our heroes at the Boulevard

The origins of rugby

William Webb Elllis couldn't dribble
So he picked up the ball and ran
And they reckon that is how
Rugby football first began

Maybe they were such rotten shots
They couldn't hit the goal
Thats why they gave two points
For kicking over a pole

And how did the ball become oval
The idea is not really sound
Maybe someone squashed a football
As it lay upon the ground

Some ideas are very confusing
And one is the rugby scrum
Now who said it was sensible
To stick your head up your team-mates bum

And while we are on the subject
There is also the maul and the ruck
It looks like disorganised mayhem
Even if you go by the book

Of course that's only for rugby union
In league we have better strategies
Playing the ball and stuff like that
Make for entertaining Saturdays

Union tends to be played by the gentry
From Twickers they issue forth
But League is a much better game
And its played by real men up north !!

Boulevard Farewell

We knew we had to move on
And the KC is the best of its kind
But we left our hearts at the Boulevard
Our home for time out of mind

We watched from the Threepenny Stand
Or from the Gordon Street end
Transferred to Best Stand if it rained
But we always stood among friends

We cheered when our lads crossed the line
And cheered when they made an offload
We cheered when they scored a conversion
And as passes seamlessly flowed

We watched in bad years and good
And at times we had glory days
We watched in rain, hail or snow
And prayed for winning ways

There's a story that's told of the day
When our time at the Boulevard ended
After the last game had finished
There was a ceremony for those who attended

There stood a Scottish piper
On the ground that had seen it all
And he played our song to the crowd
As old memories were recalled

It is said as Old Faithful was played
On a day that was strangely so still
Came blowing through the ground
A gust of wind so cold and chill

Was it players and fans from the past
Who in ghostly masses came
And were they sending a silent salute
To the spiritual heart of our game

A shiver came over the crowd
Tears glistened in many an eye
Tough blokes wept where they stood
As we said our last goodbye

It was a strange and eerie moment
Saying farewell with such sorrow
When we left our hearts at the Boulevard
And set our faces toward tomorrow

Jack Harrison VC

This son of Hull from Southcoates Lane
A Boulevard hero many tries to his name
With Billy Batten he thrilled the fans
Chanting his name all over the ground

The western front and a morning in May
The East Yorkshire Pals pinned down where they lay
A machine gun emplacement, heavy fire from the gun
A lone figure stands and begins his run

Did he think he was at the Boulevard
When he jinked and ran fast and hard
This winger weaving and running his best
Across no man's land to a machine gun nest.

That fatal day in Oppy Wood
When he gave his life for the common good
As in his brain the blood thundered loud
Did he hear the roar of the Boulevard crowd

Did he see the line at the Airlie Street end
And instead of enemies did he see friends
No pistol or grenade just a rugby ball packed
No German sniper just the Wigan full back
Did he aim for the line between the sticks
To ground the ball just right for the kick

But he silenced the gun that spat deadly fire
And it ended his life down in the French mire

And as the ref blew his whistle for time
Jack Harrison crossed that eternal line
A hero from the Boulevard he won his VC
So I learned in childhood at my grandfather's knee.

Boulevard Heaven

Is there a Boulevard up in heaven
And is it just the same
And is it always a Saturday
And is there always a game?

The team is made up of our lads
Those players once young and strong
And the supporters are the faithful
Who now are dead and gone

Billy Batten is playing at centre
In the forwards is lovely Mick Scott
Dave Topliss is the captain
And at fullback is Steve Prescott.

Jack Harrison is on one wing
And Sully on the other
In the second row are the Drake twins
Tommy Harris is the hooker.

The best stand is full to bursting
And the terraces filled with fans
While the lads are singing Old Faithful
All over the threepenny stand

And it's always warm and sunny
It never hails or rains
The ref is blind in one eye
And not over-endowed with brains.

And in this part of heaven
The away team is often Leeds
Cos they hate to come to Boulevard
And get hammered to their knees.

In the eternal directors box
The Challenge Cup is proudly shown
In heaven we got it at Wembley
From someone close to the throne

If there's a Boulevard up in heaven
Well that would be really nice
As we shout "Come on you Hull"
On the terraces of paradise.

Stan Cowan

I heard today that he had died
Passed from this world and gone on his way
A familiar name, a remembered face
Aged 83 so the newspapers say

It is years since last I thought of him
He played for us when young and strong,
Now his smiling face on an old photograph
Is all that remains of those days long gone

We loved him then and chanted his name
Cheering pass or tackle or catch
Talked of his speed in pubs and bars
His name on our lips each week at the match

We knew him so well for all those years
Then he hung up his boots and left without trace
He lived his life and became an old man
While younger players took his place

Then I read today that he had died
And I was shocked to recall him again
I'd not thought of him for many a year
But I remembered once more that familiar name

And I shed a tear for days that are gone
When we shouted his name at our favourite place
And I bade farewell to that Boulevard lad
Once young and strong with a smiling face

Stan Cowan played on the wing for Hull FC in the Fifties and Sixties. He died in February 2015

Challenge Cup

I remember the glory days
As we played in the Challenge Cup
The feeling of mounting excitement
As the final rounds came up.

The first time the cup came home
We beat Wakefield in 1914
The final was held at Halifax
For so many the last game they'd see

In 82 we won against Widnes
Though it took a replay to decide
Elland Road was the scene of our triumph
The place where we regained our pride

And in Cardiff in 20 05
After a triumphant and glorious run up
Hull FC beat Leeds in the final
And walked off with the Challenge Cup

They say we are jinxed at Wembley
We can't win when we're playing there
But as all true fans will tell you
We're sure to win it next year

And we will sing Old Faithful
As we play in the Challenge Cup
And we'll have that mounting excitement
As the final rounds come up

We'll win the treasured trophy
Before a mighty assembly
Gareth Ellis will lift it high
And we'll get it from the Queen ... at Wembley

Sammy Lloyd

When they come to write the story
In a hundred years or more
And they tell of Boulevard heroes
Of those who went before.

They will write of that legendary side
That Hull FC employed
And they will write in letters of gold
Of Knocker Norton and Sammy Lloyd

A second row forward for Classy Cas
With retirement on his mind
Sammy got the call from Hull FC
And without hesitation he signed

When Sammy came to the Boulevard
It only seemed to be right
That a bloke with all that charisma
Should be wearing the black and white

Scoring fourteen goals from as many attempts
On his famous debut appearance
Kicking goals from all over the Boulevard
In a record-breaking performance

The first year that he played for us
78-79 was the season
We won every match, lost nary a one
A record that cannot be beaten

Those surely were the glory years
The team wrote the record books
I remember Dave Topliss and Charlie Stone
The Kiwi's, Vince Farrar, Lee Crooks

Arthur Bunting at the helm
The lads carried our banner high
A tight knit unit sweeping all before
More stars than the stars in the sky

That wonderful world-class side
Sammy played a pivotal part
Knocker Norton was the general
Huge fan base at its heart

Sammy signed up for just one season
Stayed five years in the end
Then he hung up his boots to the fans regret
Cos we knew we had lost a friend

And when they come to write the story
In a hundred years or more
And they tell of Boulevard heroes
Of those who went before

They will write of that famous side
That Hull FC employed
And they will write in letters of gold
Of a legend called Sammy Lloyd

Threepenny Stand

A ramshackle construction even when it was new
It was feared all over the land
Of legendary fame throughout the game
The notorious Threepenny Stand.

The comments they gave and the racket they made
The noise could have wakened the dead
The support our lads had in good times and bad
Was worth ten points it is said

To welcome away teams the tunnel was caged
To shield and protect their fellas
As the roof was whacked and the bars attacked
By old ladies with umbrellas

Under the stand it was like Niagara
As blokes had a half time wee
And the reek of the place brought tears to your face
Stale tobacco, old beer and strong pee

It was an unforgettable mighty sound
Boulevard in vocal bombard
Singing Old Faithful and Come on you Hull
Or just shouting "gerem onside"

A ramshackle construction even when it was new
It was feared all over the land
Of legendary fame throughout the game
The notorious Threepenny Stand.

Lament for a Lost Player

For a few measly quid that's why he left us
Just a few bob to stick in his coat
Went to a place where we couldn't follow
Went where we didn't want him to go.

Agents and lawyers had studied his contract
Found a small loophole just waiting in lieu
They calmly said that contract's not binding
No compensation is therefore due

Our club had trained him, coached him, nurtured him
We on the terraces worshipped his name
That is all gone now, now that he's left us
All that remains is hatred and blame

He'll never be ours again, never be welcomed
The lad that we loved and who kept us enthralled
We shouted his name, chanted over and over
Now if he returns it's to whistles and calls

So let us forget him now, let us start over
Pick a new player with courage and dash
We called him traitor when he followed the silver
Crossing city and county in search of the cash

And in a few years when we're looking backward
We'll mention once more that dishonoured name
And recall how we worshipped the brilliant lad
Who brought us such sadness, sorrow and shame

For a few measly quid that's why he left us
Just a few bob to stick in his coat
Went to a place where we couldn't follow
Went where we didn't want him to go.

Over the years a few players have left the club under acrimonious circumstances. This poem does not apply to any particular player.

Ted Capes

When I was little I had an uncle
Well he was only an uncle of sorts
He was really a friend of my grandad
And he was very well up on sports.

Uncle Ted was a prison officer
At a time when life was hard
And though from the east of the city
He attended the Boulevard

He really loved Hull FC
And that's no exaggeration
He was a fanatical supporter
You could say it was a fixation

When walking up Holderness Road
As he was going to work
He would cross to the other side
Thus avoiding Craven Park

And when we lost in the Yorkshire Cup
In the final so it is said
He was so depressed on return
He just went straight to bed

He turned his face to the wall
And wouldn't eat or speak
His wife could do nothing with him
He stayed there for a week

I guess in the end he got up
To go back to work at the prison
And thought (like the rest of the fans)
There is always another season

When he got old he had to move north
To go and live with his son
But he left his heart at the Boulevard
When all was said and done

When I was little I had an uncle
Who was mad about Hull FC
And I loved that kind old man
Who meant a lot to me

He lived for Rugby league
And that's no exaggeration
He was a fanatical supporter
With a black and white fixation.

The Faithful

When Hull supporters congregate
And banter ebbs and flows
There are often conversations
About games played years ago.

And they talk of yesterday's heroes
And of players good and bad
They discuss games won and lost
And of the times we had

But there is one game we never mention
When we realised all our fears
That game we don't speak of at all
It's a sadness too deep for tears

And late on that desolate day
When we tasted such bitter defeat
At midnight I heard tired fans
Sing Old Faithful in an East Hull street

And that's why we are The Faithful
And aye that is the rub
We sing even when we get beat
And we are loyal to our club

And that's what it means to support
To be there in bad days and good
To cheer when we win and sing when we lose
Because the team is in our blood

The Boulevard 2015

It is only a battered old street
That once saw better days
The heart of a strong community
In many different ways

It started off rather posh
With houses designed for the gentry
But over time the area declined
As we moved through the twentieth century

You may think that you are in France
The name has a Parisian connection
But just listen to the people
Speaking with a Hull inflexion

When it was built it must have been something
With ladies in Edwardian dress
Strolling with immaculate gentlemen
Past villas designed to impress

And tucked away down Airlie Street
It was there you would have found
Even in those days long gone
That famous rugby ground

Sadly it's all changed now
The Boulevard has urban blight
And the rugby ground is an Academy
Devoted to educational might

But sometimes on an autumn evening
You get a feeling of times gone by
And the splendour of that avenue
Is there just beyond your eye

So listen very carefully
For you might catch the sound
Of a carriage travelling by
Or a murmur from the rugby ground

It is only a battered old street
That once saw better days
But occasionally time passes by
In strangely different ways.

Old Faithful

It started very early
Grandad's love of Hull FC
He was six when he first went to Boulevard
In nineteen hundred and three

He loved Hull with a singular passion
I am sure it was his life force
He saw the world in black and white
Irregular stripes of course

He liked every kind of sport
Thought athletics and cricket were grand
And he loved to see horses racing
Went to meetings all over the land

But the Airlie birds always came first
His eyes shone as he told the tale
Of watching them win at Boulevard
Or despairing when sometimes they failed

When he walked down the aisle with Grandma
There was a reception after you see
At half past two all the men walked out
Because Hull kicked off at three

No bridegroom, best man or friends
No fathers or brothers and worse
The women looked at each other and shrugged
"Should have checked the fixture list first"

He was a quiet and gentle man
With a single passion in life
In his world Hull FC was always up there
Just behind his children and wife

And when he came to the end
He was confused and his memory gone
You could always coax a smile
When you told him that Hull had won

He passed his passion for rugby league
To his children and their children too
Which is why I am standing here
Explaining it all to you

It started very early
Grandad's love of Hull FC
He was six when he first went to Boulevard
In nineteen hundred and three

Fishing

Terry Ireland

Three Day Millionaires

I'm a deckie on a side winder
A rough and brutal life
Which is sometimes reflected in
The way I treat my family and wife.

And the fast blacks queue for me
Eager to take my trade
And the pubs welcome me for
Their share of what I've made.

And they say we are heroes,
Us of the deep sea fishing fleet
In our powder blue suits with
Brothel creepers on our feet.

Three day millionaires they call us
But do they ever stop to think
Why I fill my life ashore
With company and drink.

Sometimes when the catch is low
Or when the market price is bad
I owe the owners money when they
Claim back allowances the family had;

Then we exist on the tallyman,
Or, what I really hate,
Beg at Myton Street Social
For a hand out from the state.

Three days between trips
Three days to try and live
Then it's back on board where
They take all I have to give.

Seventeen fisher lives gone
For every miner's life lost
All for cheap fish and taties;
Do they add that to the cost.

I'm a deckie on a sidewinder, which
Can be a seaborne life of hell
But when the catch is good boys
Me and my family live so well.

The average shore time between fishing trips was three days. During this time, if it had been a successful trip, their pockets were awash with money and freely spent. Hence their nickname "Three Day Millionaires"

Big Lil - 1968

It was a year of revolutions
Worldwide, quiet little fights
Wanting more from democracy
Fighting for Civil Rights.
From Hull three trawlers sank
February, fifty eight lives lost,
Adding to that 10 thousand
Deep sea fishing would finally cost.

They called them Headscarf Heroes
Big Lil lead the housewives, the few
Who stood and fought for
More safety for the crews.
They marched on Downing Street
In defence of their men
Met with Premier Harold Wilson
Up there at Number 10;

United the fishing community
All over the land,
Brought the fight to the public,
Made an historic stand
To fight for basic safety
To fight for better ways
For the men who fished each year
On average over three hundred days.

She was vilified and attacked
Received letters threatening death
But Big Lil and her companions
Fought with their every breath.

They won many concessions
At their personal cost
The efforts of these ladies
Saved many lives from being lost.

The fishing fleet is finished.
Old Hessle Road is gone.
In time and at a price
This City has moved on.
Such an historic figure
I find it such an awful shame
So very few know or remember
Big Lil Bilocca's name.

Jonesy

I saw the scar down his calf
long smooth and white
standing out against his tan
in the bright summer light;

whisky surgery he told me,
seeing my curious glance
and I got him talking
while I had the chance.

We both settled down with a beer
and he told me how it had been
just so casually describing, to me,
an horrific dangerous scene.

Fishing in a storm off Iceland
trawling for the cod
risking their lives
under a fickle sea god.

Then the steel warp parted
catching just him alone,
whipping back to gash his leg
right down to the bone.

The whisky forced down him
until he really didn't care,
the skipper producing a needle
to sew him up then and there.

And the crew carried on fishing
with no time to waste
every second's fishing necessary
in the profit's chase.
He said it really didn't hurt
with the whisky in his gob
and he reckoned the skipper
had done quite a neat job.

Very soon after that
he decided to come ashore,
said the lure of the sea
didn't pull so much anymore,

and with a wife and child
didn't want to push his luck.
As an ex deckie he fairly easily
obtained his docker's book.

A very quiet person,
very pleasant and shy
but I go to know him well
as the years rolled by.

Never again mentioned his leg
which I only saw by chance,
that long smooth white scar
having just caught my glance.

Post Cod War Blues – Epitaph

It's by the old lock gates
and not so easily found,
there on the bull nose
if you know your way around:
a very modest monument,
spare compact and neat,
tribute to the lost of our
deep sea trawler fleet.

It's just a few feet away
from that very place,
the entrance to the Humber,
where they joined frantic race
to bring to the nation
their very favourite dish,
the harvest of the sea,
cheap, tasty, fresh wet fish.

Though it's never admitted,
in the heart of the Cold war
as well as their fishing
that fleet did so much more,
spying on the Russians
at a possible great cost,
for to be caught meant
maybe ships and lives lost.

Now among some dereliction
There are still working docks
Plying very different trades
Through very different locks;

there's still the new fish market
now tucked quietly away,
scant reminder of the past
when King Cod ruled the day.

The grey stone memorial,
small, stern and austere,
the site of a remembrance
held once every year,
while the Humber as ever
rolls on down to the sea
in silent reminder of
how things used to be.

Biography

He loved those special days
When the incoming sea
Reached its high water
For afternoon tea,
When he'd sit on his balcony,
Solitary master and host,
And raise his cup to Neptune
In most respectful toast.

He'd sit and remember
With a rueful pride
Slipping past the Bullnose
To sail with the tide.
On to the North Sea, on
To trawl Icelandic cod
Braving the moods of
Those fickle sea gods.

Twenty years later
At just thirty five,
Still deep sea fishing
And still alive,
He'd finally decided
To bring his sea legs ashore.
He'd had enough.
He'd not fish anymore.

And for the rest of his time
Had worked on the docks
Almost in sight of
Those old fishing locks.
Now feeling the cold and
Time to go back inside
Lifted his glass in salute
To the still flowing tide.

To Skipper Pete

Today I walked the Humber Bank
Across the old locks
On in the grey drizzle
Through the old town docks;
Normally a solitary walk but
Today I happened to meet
An ex trawler skipper from
Our old deep sea fishing fleet.

He told me the fleet still existed
If it could still be called as such
For its remnants and quota were
Mostly owned by Iceland and the Dutch.
He talked of the Cod War sell out
That meant the industry couldn't last
So the Hull fishing fleet became
A redundant thing of the past.

And of the treatment of workers,
Used as labour that came cheap
Then with little compensation
Just dumped on the scrap heap.
He said it had been years
Since he'd been down this way
But had been up town and by impulse
Had walked through here today

He was struck by the desolation
Of this area he'd known as a lad
I don't think he'd realised that
The dereliction was quite so bad.
Standing atop the fish house roofs
I listened avidly to his talk.
Then with so much food for thought
Continued on to finish my walk,

Past the derelict landing piers
Just off the bank,
Timbers breaking the water
In parallel ranks,
Like combat veterans on
A Remembrance Day parade
Or just another reminder of
Maritime lost jobs and trade

Post Cod War Blues Part 1

St Andrews fish dock has long closed down
and there's no longer a fleet to sail from the town
the old lock gates where the trawlers would queue
to land for the markets are no longer used

a metalled road runs over the lock
and no water runs between river and dock
buildings are tumbled or been razed to the ground
and it's quiet and eerie with only the sounds

of the water and wind and shrieks of the gulls
this Sunday morning in the old docks of Hull
it's forlorn and deserted and so cold and bleak
I'll cuddle the fire for the rest of the week

but I need to watch it as it finally goes
I need to remember so my kids will know
they've filled one dock in with mud and sand
there's probably a subsidy for reclaiming land

and thrown up warehouses and the usual shops
to erase our past so one history stops
there's a bowling alley to practice ten-pin
and as much fast food as you can cram in

this is the future and it's brash and it's bold
this is the era of grab all you can hold.
it's taken my city and torn out it's soul
for there's no pride in claiming the dole

they say this is progress and progress is all
so bugger the memories of those on the Gaul
and bugger the hardships and bugger the pain
and bugger the families who'll never see again

the pride and the swagger of the trawler wage earner
or the newly wise eyes of the young deckie learner
there's no more last beers and fast taxi rides
to board from the lock as she sails with the tide

now it's heaven bless the poor
and heaven bless the sick
and heaven bless the slow
and heaven bless the thick
and heaven bless those with their backs to the wall
whilst for the few winners it's bugger you all

Fishgate Market

Six hundred years of history
Wiped out at last.
What connection now has our city
With its long fishing past?
Wrecked trawler company offices
Lined around silted docks
With a footpath running across
Dilapidated St Andrew's locks.

An old trawler moored on the Hull
Part of the new museum scene
One of the few reminders that
The industry has ever been.
A monument to the dead
Still stands on the Bullnose
Fishgate stands across the dock
But yesterday it was closed.

It's been moved to Grimsby
To the river's other shore
And Hull as a fishing city
Is finally no more.
In the city centre universal shops
Have been thrown up there;
We have become a cardboard city
That could be any town anywhere.

Post Cod War Blues - A mouthful of ashes

Blood money isn't paid in silver these days,
just transferred straight to your account
with a sheet of computerised data
to tell you their agreed amount.

I'm standing over the fish sheds,
to my front near empty docks,
behind, the steady running Humber,
to the left the gates and the locks.

In my pocket this little piece of paper
telling me the price of my pride
and I'm standing out here in the open
'cos I won't be seen crying inside.

So many years I served on those trawlers
the boy to man years of my life
I saw so much more of my ship mates
than I did of my children and wife;

stood on the decks in the cold and the fog
and the rain and the sleet and the ice
gutting the fish for your table.
We accepted it wouldn't be nice.

I worked all those years for a living
because fishing was part of my blood
from a proud and vital community
surviving both bad years and good

Most of those years worked for one company,
most of that time in one or two ships
I was a regular deckie
I didn't miss many trips.

Then they turned and told me you're finished
with a little just by the way
you were only a casual worker,
don't get any severance pay.

All these years we've fought for our justice.
For recognition of our effort and pride,
The numbers slowly dwindling.
One by one old comrades died:

And now they call this a victory
time to pay for my wasted years
so I'm standing atop of this fish shed
no shame in my bitter tears.

enjoy your cod my brother
But grant me one little wish
Before you add your vinegar
Just think of one price paid for fish.

Lunch At The Sailmakers

Sitting in the warmth looking over the river
Where my darts partner, Bernard used to work
When they did once make sails and tarpaulins
Before it became a pub where we could lurk
After our short walk along the waterfront:
Desolation and dereliction have moved on.
Many of the old chandlers and merchants
Premise are now very nearly gone.

Bare rafters outlined against a grey sky
As tiles and bricks have been cast around
To lie where they gradually fell, to join
More obstacles on the littered ground,
Easily avoided as we wander almost aimlessly
Surprised at how the decay has speeded,
As though it represents a past, the memory
Of which is no longer valued or needed.

The once splendid Lord Line offices stand,
Glassless windows, like blinded eyes seem
To survey the old, silted, grassed over dock
As though locked in the thrall of a dream
When the lock gates worked, letting trawlers in
To land the slippery, silver, gutted fish,
To be then sold and shipped nationwide,
Once the nation's favourite cheap dish.

(Not the same need for freshness
Not the same need to hurry
As fish and chips fall prey
To boiled rice and Indian curry).
Here the bobbers manhandled the crates
In wooden clogs, steel toed footwear,
Hard wearing, light and ideally suited
For the work done around there.

These clogs clattering,
The steel toes casting a spark
At times to quickly disappear
In the early morning, pre dawn dark
This rich heritage, lacking care
Cannot much longer last,
As though the City is
Ashamed of its fishing past.

So we return to The Sailmakers,
In our dreams maybe alone
As teens leave the door unclosed and
Chat away on the essential mobile phone
Or smoke their cigarettes, now banned,
Inside in public places in what is now left
Of our once free and carefree land.
We have thrown out baby and bath water

In our rush to so called progress
Not seeming to realise we possess more
Materially, but spiritually, so much less.
Through the slow closing doors
Slowly seeps the January cold:
Maybe I am redundant,
As I grey and grow inexorably old.
The shade of ever laughing Bernard seems
To hover here, as though watching me try,
And nearly always failing, so we lose
As my dart misses that elusive Bullseye.

Sidewinder Blues

Through lock gates
Landing with the tide
Fast Black waiting
At the dock side
Had a good trip
Don't know what I'll get
But I'm sure i've not
Again landed in debt.

Powder blue suit
Bell bottom trews
Slim Jim tie
Brothel creeper shoes
Few pints at Rayners
A few more up town
Belly to the bar
No time to sit down.

Three Day Millionaires
Pockets all a jingle
Just three days
To socialise and mingle
Chatting up the birds
No real time to flirt
Can't beat a pint with
Arm round a bit of skirt

A few more hours
Then back at sea
A Fisherman's life
That's the life for me
On a sidewinder
Some times not so nice
Fighting the weather
Fighting the ice.

Thinking of the bundle
I hope I'll have made
Thinking of the booze
And thinking of getting laid
Through the lock gates
Landing with the tide
Fast Black waiting
At the dock side.

Lord Line

The 'dozers have been in
Ripping history apart
Clearing those old buildings
So redevelopment can start.

The old Lord Line building,
Part derelict and now alone
Looks so much sadder
As it stands there on its own.

Once a place of pride but now
Overlooking a silted dock,
Half filled in for a shopping park,
And the remains of St Andrew's lock,

Whose historic gates have been left to rot
So they are barricaded by barbed wire
To close the right of way across
As the layers of mud rise higher and higher.

The White Fish Authority
That was once housed there,
A not too old edifice,
Is gradually sliding into disrepair.

This a vandalism by neglect
A modern developers' crime
Making preservation unlikely and
Uneconomic with the passage of time.

This could have been a peoples' park
A celebration of a prosperous past.
But there is no time for sentiment
And commerce has won at last.
What monstrosities will they throw up
In profit and losses name?
To me its a monstrous sin
To them just a continuing game.

They had the patience to
Bide their time and wait
Then send the 'dozers in
When conservation was too late.

All poems in this book are subject to © Sue Houlston and Terry Ireland 2015

ALL RIGHTS RESERVED This book contains material protected under Copyright Laws. Any unauthorized reprint or use of this material is prohibited. No part of this book may be reproduced or transmitted in any form or by any means, electronic or mechanical, including photocopying, recording or by any information storage and retrieval system without express written permission from the author.